Who Should...?

Norma Kennedy, Doug Ramsay, and Pat Shields

Who should clean up after me
when I have made a mess?

It's up to me.

It's *my* responsibility.

Who should try to help someone who feels hurt or sad?

It's up to me.

It's *my* responsibility.

Who should help around the house and finish all my jobs?

It's up to me.

It's *my* responsibility.

Who should keep the outdoors clean by using garbage cans?

It's up to me.

It's *my* responsibility.

Who should try to be on time
and not make people wait?

It's up to me.

It's *my* responsibility.

Who should know the rules at school
and try hard to keep them?

It's up to me.

It's *my* responsibility.

Who should always tell the truth when something has gone wrong?

It's up to me.

It's *my* responsibility.

Who should try to make our world
the best that it can be?

Our World Is Our Responsibility.

It's up to us.

It's *our* responsibility.